The Unluckiest Man in the World

and Similar Disasters

Mike Harding

Illustrated by Bill Tidy

Arrow Books

Arrow Books Limited
62-65 Chandos Place, London, WC2N 4NW

An imprint of Century Hutchinson Limited

London Melbourne Sydney Auckland
Johannesburg and agencies throughout
the world

First published in Great Britain by Robson Books Ltd 1979
Arrow edition 1980
Reprinted 1981, 1982, 1984 (twice), 1985 and 1987

All songs and music copyright © 1979 Moonraker Music
Ltd/EMI Music Ltd. All other material copyright © 1979
Mike Harding/Moonraker Production Ltd with the exception
of 'Ackroyd's Funeral' and 'Bring on the Rosy-Cheeked
Girls' which are copyright © 1979 EMI Music Ltd.

This book is sold subject to the condition that it shall not,
by way of trade or otherwise, be lent, re-sold, hired out,
or otherwise circulated without the publisher's prior consent
in any form of binding or cover other than that in which it is
published and without a similar condition including this
condition being imposed upon the subsequent purchaser.

Set in Linoterm Times by Rugcliffe Ltd, Cuckfield, Sussex

Printed and bound in Great Britain by
Anchor Brendon Limited, Tiptree, Essex

ISBN 0 09 923540 4

Contents

Preface

I first met Mike Harding at the Edinburgh Festival in 1973. He had just won the Albert Tatlock look-alike contest with honours. Since then his material has gone steadily down hill. By far the funniest man in England (you'll notice I didn't say Britain), Mike Harding, like superfluous hair, grows on you. I look on his book with admiration and not a little jealousy.

BILLY CONNOLLY

Mike Harding

Mike Harding was born on 23 October 1944 in the picturesque spa of Lower Crumpsall, Manchester. His early years were spent in the shadow of a dark, satanic cream-cracker factory where his family had worked for years designing chocolate fingers and punching the holes in jammy dodgers. By the age of two he could recite the entire works of Milton by heart but by the time he was three, he'd forgotten them all.

His father at that time was Head Keeper at Hanky Park, the estate of the Earl of Salford, and his mother was lady-in-waiting to Elsie Scrote of 24 Sebastopol Terrace. His grandmother, on his mother's side, had been a gas mantle knitter and amateur maggot wrestler before marrying his grandfather on his return from Australia, after he had been transported to Botany Bay for stealing cat's eyes out of the road. His grandfather, Sigismund J. Gropesworthy, was generally known as Manchester's most unsuccessful criminal. Apparently, he had sent away for a pamphlet called 'Teach Yourself to Burgle,' advertised in what was known then as *Young Moore's Almanac*. Of the three pages, only pages one and three arrived, as a result of which he would walk backwards in shops shouting 'Hands up! This is a getaway!'

The family fortunes began to dwindle after the failure of the condensed milk nut harvest in Lower Weaste in 1927 following a summer so wet that half the population in Manchester was found to have sprouted gills.

meant that the family seat in Rickett's buildings had to be sold with all its effects, comprising four tea chests, a bed, a hand-carved effigy of Florence Nightingale made entirely from one piece of Co-op lard, and a map showing the travels of Mungo Park. The family was forced to move then into a modest two-roomed bus shelter in Harpurhey.

At the age of five he started at the school of St Dunstan the Aggressive in Lower Crumpsall where his career was soon marked by a show of academic brilliance demonstrated in his ability to make plasticine worms and find his own way to the toilet without ending up in the stock cupboard. His model of Blackpool Tower made entirely from curdled school milk was unfortunately lost to posterity. However, he was expelled from St Dunstan's at the age of five-and-a-half after the teacher discovered that he had secreted a copy of *The Perfumed Garden* inside the cover of a Janet and John reader. This would never have been discovered had he not absent-mindedly followed his neighbour reading aloud 'See Fluff, see Fluff chase the ball' with 'He ripped the flimsy silk from off her swelling bosom and thrust himself panting into her arms.'

He then continued his educational career at Inkerman Street Primary School Atheists Mixed Infants, which was run on the Pestalozzi principle since most of the staff usually were. By the time he left that school he had a reading age of minus two and could count up to ten, jack, queen, king and ace. He had also been voted 'The Boy with the Coldest Hands in the School' by the Sheila O'Rourke Bike Shed Amateur Tactile Appreciation Society. It was at this time also that Sheila O'Rourke displaced Santa Claus, Batman and 'Where does the water in the tap come from?' as subjects that dominated his waking consciousness. He was expelled from Inkerman Street for turning up one morning in nothing but his vest thinking that he was in one of his own nightmares. The rest of his education was acquired at his grandmother's knee, which she painted black and wrote on with chalk.

Following this undistinguished academic career, at the age of seventeen he bought a set of Mongolian bagpipes and joined a rock and roll band which, unfortunately, folded after all the other members had nervous breakdowns. He then bought an electric guitar and joined a Mongolian bagpipe band. This too, was unsuccessful and resulted in a dispersal of the Khengis Khan Hot Five Rhythm Aces.

It was during this period of relative obscurity that he wrote his most popular works, fondly remembered pieces such as the operetta *The Cockroach Hunters*, the finished *Symphonia Salfordia*, *The Waltz of the Potatoes* from the ballet *The Magic Greengrocer* and his great opera cycle *Der Blitzenfahrt*, which was written round the legends concerning the northern gods Manfred, Siegfried, Boddington and Old Trafford. The cycle tells of how Siegfried descends into the depths of the river to talk with the Irk Maidens amongst the old bedsteads, prams and mangles. They tell him of a pot of gold kept by the Dwarfs of Rotherham, who also have the secret of the meaning of Life and have cornered the market in football boot dubbin. After a battle lasting four years and resulting in exorbitant claims in overtime from the dwarfs. Siegfried defeats them by hurling effigies of Georgie Best at them from amongst the clouds.

After writing *Der Blitzenfahrt*, he wallowed in more obscurity for several years before being rediscovered while working as a labourer on a North Sea Treacle Rig. He now lives in a council pyramid in Goole where he is working on his memoirs and growing prize dandelions.

Bill Tidy

Born 1933, Prenton, Tranmere. Moved to Liverpool in 1940 for the Blitz. Survived. Schooling at St Margarets, Anfield. Left school at 15 and became the obligatory shipping office boy. Joined the army as a regular (glorified National Serviceman) for three years and served in Germany, Korea, and joined a Liverpool advertising agency which was worse than Korea.

Took up cartooning in 1957. Contributes to *Punch*, *Private Eye* ('The Cloggies'), *Daily Mirror* ('The Fosdyke Saga'), *Titbits* ('The Sporting Spagthorpes'), BBC and ITV, advertising agencies and everyone else. Received Granada TV 'What the Papers Say' award for Cartoonist of the Year 1974.

Married sparkling Neapolitan in 1960 and now shares three children with her.

Slightly disillusioned about football in general, but still loves Everton.

Bring on the
Rosy-Cheeked Girls

My sexual awakening came at a time when a song in the Hit Parade proclaimed:

> 'She wears red feathers and a hulu skirt
> She wears red feathers and a hulu skirt
> She lives on just coconuts and fish from the sea.'

I always swore that if I met this woman I would marry her since she promised to be both exciting and cheap to feed. Since then I've looked for her wherever I've been, but all to no avail. Still she lingers on in the dark corners of my imagination as being firm of flesh, dark of skin and constantly smiling. And so would you be if you had to walk round looking like the roof of a Kafir's hut.

There's something about people who smile. Freud always said that someone who smiles has had his ego tickled by the cosmos. Jung, however, put it down to acid indigestion. I believe there are people who are positive and generally happy all the time. These people are nearly all locked up. Most of us are happy most of the time, some of us are miserable most of the time. If you stand on a street corner for long enough you can see the miserable ones passing by, their faces set in a scowl, plodding along determinedly as though wading through a lake of scrambled eggs. Life is jaded for them, each morning holds no hope, no promise, just the prospect of another day the same as every other, grey and meaningless. But not everybody's an accountant. There are other worthwile jobs that can be found that are of a benefit to mankind and give the worker a sense of self-fulfilment – jobs like canning lettuce, or being a diesel oil taster, or the man who says the pips on the GPO Time Signal.

Such a man was Enrico Longbottom, who shot from the oblivion of the rat race into holding down the job of Head Wine Waiter at the Inn On The Park Hotel, Bacup, after he had been Maître d'Hôtel for fourteen years at the Waldorf Astoria, Oswaldthwistle. Enrico found it impossible to look on the black side since it would have been too dark and he had broken his glasses anyway. He was as jolly as the day is long which is not very long in Bacup since the sun sets there at half-past-one in the afternoon. Yet nothing made him miserable, lest it be the sight of a pair of mating dugongs. And as such a sight is rare in Bacup, he tended on the whole to be happy and contented. When Enrico entered a room it lit up, mainly because he was the only one who knew where the switch was.

Enrico's greatest ambition was to be a writer. He wrote books such as *Treasure Island* and *Kidnapped,* which was a bit of a waste of time since Robert Louis Stevenson had already written them. He also wrote *Withering Tights,* a story of a love affair which took place on the Yorkshire moors and was later made into a film with Scarlett O'Hara playing Dirk Bogarde and Ernest Borgnine playing John Wayne. As a result of which Ernest Borgnine played Scarlett O'Hara in the finals of the West Riding Hedgehog Juggling competition.

Enrico was also responsible for coining the immortal phrase 'Lily, 14 Paradise Street – Paradise, 14 Lily's Street'. He also made a film about drunk rabbits called *Water It Down,* and a sex novel called *Topic of Rotherham.* His most famous novel, however, of all time, and the follow-up to the books that made his name – *The Trumpeting Major* and *Jude the Obscene* – was, of course, *Mad from the Farting Crowds*. He died at the age of ninety-three and left his body to medical science. It was used as a door-stop at the Manchester Royal Infirmary Ear, Nose, Throat, Ankle and Dandruff Department.

Bring on the Rosy-Cheeked Girls

Bring on the rosy-cheeked girls,
The smiling ones, the light-footed dancers,
Those that sing with their eyes,
Those with the warm breasts and soft hands,
Those that look deep in the eyes,
Not at the garbage of garb.
Bring on the dark, the fair, the brown as a berry,
Bring them all on with their wet laughing mouths,
The fat, the thin, the short, and the lanky,
But let them be filled of life as a pod with peas,
Let them feel as company comfortable as an old friendly jacket,
young or old,
And most of all . . . let them be merry.

And then take all the others,
All the tight-lipped, crab-faced, mewling, mithering,
Niggardly, sour-faced, crab-mouthed,
Cold-titted, tight-arsed, moaning,
Sullen, frozen-legs-together,
Money-grubbing bitches, and
Take them and heap them together
On some blear and dreary moor
In the howling sleet
And moaning drizzle of November . . . and leave them there,
For it deserves them
And they each other.

Then bring on the lads,
The smiling lads,
The open-handed, shoulder-to-the-wheel lads,
Lame dogs helped over stiles lads,
Take a pint, stand a corner lads,
Good laughing lads,
Lads with a quart of life in their hands
And eyes that look straight . . .
Bring on the tall, the short, the long,
The runners, the walkers,
Those that can hammer, those that can turn out a song,
Bring on the fat, the thin, the bald and the hairy,
Young or old,
So long as they sup life by the gallon . . .
So long as they're merry.

Then take all the others,
The sly-eyed, twisty-mouthed grabbers and fumblers,
the shifty-faced, two-tongued, lead-swinging lizards,
The snotty-nosed, mardy-arsed bullies
And false friends . . .
And stick them up to their necks
In the foulest stink-pot of an old bog
You can find . . . head down . . .
And leave them there.

But for God's sake not to near
That moor with all the old whores . . .
If they meet up and breed
We're all buggered.

Mr Fat Cigar

It is a cold December night and I am in Joe's Speakeasy on the corner of 57th when the story I am about to tell you takes place. A pauper kid with a crutch is standing across the road in the sleet and the cold selling matches from a tray. It is such a night that snowmen are not coming out in, such a night that the wind is tearing off people's skin if the guy ropes are not fastened properly. There in the wet-cold sleet and wind the kid is leaning on his crutch selling matches – and not just selling matches but singing! Now if I am to say he has a great voice I would be saying the Pope is a communist, because the kid has a voice like someone tipping coke. The cold has made his voice like ripping canvas and just as loud.

Well, I am sat with Louie the Nose and Harry the Hump, talking of this and that and that and this, when we see Hiram Rippemoff riding by in his Rolls Royce Corniche.

Now Hiram Rippemoff is one member in this ville that nobody says a bad word to twice. He has so many body-guards a mobile canteen has to follow them round. He is what is called a 'theatrical agent', which is to say in street language – Barabas with a licence.

Such members as have fallen into disagreement with Hiram have afterwards been found trying to walk on the bottom of the river in concrete galoshes, a sport that nobody is ever going to win prizes for. Hiram's hobby at this time is throwing hot cigar butts into puddles at paupers' feet and pulling the wings off Boeing 707s.

Well, as Hiram passes the singing matchseller kiddy he throws a big cigar butt out of the window of the Rolls Royce which hits the kid's tray of matches and sets them alight. The crutch catches fire and the kid is almost burnt to the ground and is good and mad at this, but Hiram just laughs as the kid howls in all the cold and sleet. Then Hiram notices that the kid, as he howls, is hitting high C in a soprano voice – but like with Satchmo's tone of voice!!! It is a voice such as no one has heard in this neighbourhood of the burgh and results in several nervous breakdowns and improved business for glaziers within three or four miles.

Hiram Rippemoff I see light another cigar, step out of the limousine and address the kid thus:

'Hey kid! I can make you a star!!'

'No kiddin', Mister?' said the kid. 'I ain't got no props. Mister, I ain't got no band, no music, nothin'.'

'That's OK,' says Hiram, 'we'll do the show right here. You ever heard of Svengali?'

'No,' says the kid. 'What does he play?'

'Forget it, kid, just sing.'

So the kid sings *Ave Maria* till the street is full of crying Mafia and goes on to sing *Danny Boy* till the street is full of crying Irish cops which results in a crying shoot-out; and with bodies dropping all around them, Hiram signs the kid up for a million-dollar contract and bills him:

PAUPER JOE THE MATCHSELLER
The kid with a voice like
a choir of angels with chainsaws

So in a few hours Hiram hires the Carnegie Hall for a year; he invests every single sou, every clod in the kid's future, even the dirt from under his finger-nails (and such dirt! five guineas an ounce, straight off Duchesses'

backs!). Hiram hocks his cars, his yachts, his two mansions in the Bronx and his holiday home in Acapulco. He even decides which island he's going to buy with his millions – Australia.

Well, the first night, the hall is packed; they're sitting in the ashtrays, hanging from the balconies, they're trying to sneak in through the ventilators, they have to throw out three hundred ice cream girls with moustaches and hairy legs; every show biz critic in town is there with his pencil in his hand and every one of them is shutting the door on his brain with all the free booze Hiram has thrown down their necks. There they sit, waiting for the kid to sock it to them. The lights dim, the theatre hushes, an atmosphere such as you find at executions fills the hall. The excitement you can cut with a knife.

The kid has been living in the Waldorf Astoria for a month, he has a new suit of rags such as has been designed by some Frenchman flown over specially, a handmade crutch and a sequined match-tray. The stage gradually lightens; the backdrop is the Manhattan skyline, real rain falls on the stage, real winos and derelicts are falling about all over the props, a regiment of nuns is humming softly. Here comes the kid, limping on as the orchestra saw their way through the introduction to *Ave Maria*.

The kid opens his mouth – the world waits – and out comes – nothing, zilch! An ordinary voice! His cold has gone, thr's no angels, no Satchmo, no chainsaws, just ordinary Joe Voice; if he sang *Buddy, Can I Give You A Dime?* nobody would stop and listen. After two numbers people are leaving, after three they are throwing things, after four they're throwing up, after the fifth number the place is empty and the cleaners are sweeping up while the kid's half-way through *Won't You Buy My Pretty Flowers?*

24

The rest is History. Hiram Ripemoff is ruined and kills himself by taking an overdose of old Sinatra contracts, while the kid goes back to selling matches and coughing, and for once everyone is pleased at the happy way it all ends.

And if you don't believe that's a happy ending ask Sid Vicious, Janis Joplin, Jimmy Hendrix, Keith Moon, Elvis Presley, Jim Morrison, Brian Jones.

The Unluckiest Man in the World used to buy suits and wait for them to come back into fashion.

The Unluckiest Man in the World was so frightened of being struck by lightning he wore shoes with copper spikes on the soles to give him a good earth, but was unable to walk for two years after contracting rising damp and verdigris of the legs.

Mr Fat Cigar

One day when I was buskin' outside a Bingo queue,
Stood there in the pouring rain, all that day I'd earned no pay,
I was just about to pack up and go home for the night
When a fat cigar with a man on the end came waddlin' into
  sight.

A funny little bloke in a camel hair coat was stuck on that cigar,
He said, 'I'm what you need, my boy, you're gonna go far, I'll
  make you a star,
My name is Hiram Ripemoff, in showbiz I'm renowned,
So just hold on to the bumper of me Rolls and I'll run you back
  to town.'

I ran all the way to his office in town and climbed ten flights of
  stairs,
Fought me way through a carpet, a cigar that bloke gave me to
  smoke,
I smoked that three-foot long cigar, drank six bottles of gin,
Signed a dozen contracts and spewed in the paper-bin.

He signed me on for a thousand years, the deal was ten per
  cent,
Ten per cent was all for me and ninety per cent to Hiram went.
He said he'd pay me bus fares and lend me a bob or two,
And he got me a week at the London Palladium, singing to the
  queue.

He said I could keep me cloth cap as a gimmick for a while,
Said he'd get me teeth capped so I'd smile in the latest style,
He said we'd make hit singles with plugs on the radio,
Then he measured me up for a glitter suit to wear on a TV
  show.

So now that I'm a superstar I wear a sequined suit,
A great big pair of frogskin boots, a frogskin hat, I look a right
   pratt,
Next week I go to the USA for the biggest gigs of all –
Workin' the queues at the Hollywood Bowl and at Carnegie
   Hall.

Chorus

I know who you are, Mr Fat Cigar,
With your flashy clothes, and your big car,
Mr Ten Per Cent, you want me to pay the rent
On your big house in St. John's Wood.

Mr Fat Cigar

*Call the
Night Porter*

Jazz, rock and folk musicians, jugglers, comics and entertainers have replaced trolls, goblins, bogymen, border raids and toilet-seats as the lurking phantoms of popular folklore. Mothers now frighten children to bed with such sayings as 'Get to bed or the comic will get you,' or 'Hush, here comes the vibes player!' Through the ages Musoes and Jazzers and their ilk have been a group of itinerants peddling doubtful wares and living from hand to mouthpiece as best they could, a regiment of untouchables wandering from gig to gig like mountebanks or lepers, eyed with suspicion and fear by tavern keepers, sherriffs and fathers of daughters.

A previously-undiscovered manuscript from the Ashmolean Museum, Oxford, throws some light on the attitude towards comics and entertainers that has persisted since the Middle Ages. The manuscript is in two fragments, one seemingly coming from the prologue to the *Canterbury Tales,* and the other a complete tale in itself.

From the Prologue . . .

A comique thir wasse, a rednosed fule,
Could quaf his ale and jibe with anne manne,
Whilom had been in Stoctonne at a clubbe
Which better wasse he sedde thanne Birminghamme.
All bloodwebbed were his een and baggy too,
A merry knave with ale knights face and jowels,
And whenne that his old herse a bumpe did hitte,
'Crackerjacke!' did go his noisome bowels!

31

The next fragment goes on to tell *The Comique's Tale*
. . . believed by experts to be one of the first recorded
commercial traveller jokes.

Thir was in Irelaunde a merry knave
In ladies underthinges his travels made,
This manne so ugly was and foule of face
The childern ranne when he camme to a place.
A bearde he hadde as wide as any spade
And wartes on his nose like molehills laid,
Yet though he ugly wasse like mouldie spam
As yet he wasse a lewde and lechrouse man.
It chaunced one night as he walked downe a lanne,
His old grey mare did falle against a stanne
And tumbling overe felle deed on the grounde,
And ladies underthinges spreade alle arounde.
'Alacke alas, I now have as much chaunce
As doth a one legged manne to kicke his owne erse!'
Yet as he cried out in the derke nighte
Yet throughe the derknesse spied he a great light.
A ferme thir was with buildings alle around.
'Tee hee,' quoth he, 'some lodgings will be found.
Yette how wille I finde lodginges withe this bloke
If he has heard the commercialle travelours jokkes?
I will me guise in ladies underthinges
And as a maiden give the belle a ringe!'
So as a maide with bearde and with wartes
With every step he giveth out a ferte!
So he avaunced him to the ferme gate
And gan to knocke the doore though it be late.
Eftsoons a manne cam to the doore the fermer was.
'Who is that knockes so late?' the poore manne asks.
'I am a maiden loste out on the moore
So I cam knockinge at the ferme doore.'
'I ne'er before a maide with beard and wartes
Have seene, muche lesse one that so dooth ferte,
yette come ye in and sitte by the fire
And you shall sleepe with my daughter Maria!'

And so thatte nighte the lewde and lechrouse knave
Did go uppe to the chambre withe the maide.
The maide all comely wasse and handsome too,
And ungarbed slowley alle herselfe to shewe.
This ugly man his garments offe he torne
And standen naked as the daye he bornne;
Yette as he stoode his yerde gan to rise
Untill the maid could scarce believe her eyes,
'Thoughe I a maiden bee and scarce sixteen,
Such an ugly maid as you I neer have seene,
For ugly are yee with a bearde and wartes
And with every step ye letten outte a ferte,
And what is thatte so thickke between your legges?'
'That is my thirdde legge,' the false knave saide,
'My legge is cramped and needes a tendre haunde
To make the crampe go,' said the false manne.
'Well, close thy een,' the maiden said, 'I beg,
And I will help to ease your thirde legge.'
So while he stoode with een all closely clapped
On his thirde legge a mustarde pilaster she slapped.
'Youre legge is mended soone!!' she loude did shoute,
As throughe the windowe the travelour leaped out.
'Your thirde legge is such a sturdy stumpe –
See how the plaster helped you to jumpe!!'
Yet though his thirde legge all mended wasse,
The first and second bothe were brokke, alas!
The travelour wasse never soon no more
But crawled he offe from the fermer's doore,
And by the fire whenever tales are saide
They speaken oft of that three-legged maide!

The companye did laughe at such a jeste
And yette our hoste spoke out above the reste.
'This manne did ferte at avery step he tredde
Yet ye dothe the same,' our hoste laughing said.
'Methinkes ye are the manne of which ye said.'
The comique nothinge saith but blushed red,
And lo the companye fulle loud did laugh
And stopped at an inne ome alle to quaf.

Call the Night Porter

We've seen every roundabout on the A1,
Ate in every cafe on the M6.
So many jars in old hotel bars,
So many nights we got blitzed.
We've laughed in the night when the roadies got tight
And took off their trousers and flashed;
We've got into lumber with liggers and nightmares
When knuckles and noses got smashed.

Chorus
Call the night porter to set up the beers,
Some scotch and a couple of gins.
All the long roads, the long miles from home –
Let the long night's day begin.

We've eaten junk food in Greasy Joe's Rooms,
The food set before us was ate;
Bacon like cardboard and chips like bad dreams,
And the eggs ran so much they escaped.
We've woken from breakfast when dinner-time's gone
And the kitchens were closed and shut,
With sandpaper eyes and flypaper tongues
And a mouth like a bagful of soot.

We've waited for hours while one of the band
Had a kneetremble stood in the dark,
And we laughed at the din when he fell off the bin
And a million dogs started to bark;
Had too many curries in two many hurries,
Smoked too many funny Park Drive;
And it's up in the morning, aching and yawning,
With another gig in Donny tonight.

Call the Night Porter

Sporting the Old School Tie

Fifth Form at Clegg Street Secondary Modern

Johnson scudded out of prep as a soccer boot thudded into the study door.

'Cave, chaps!!!' shouted the Fat Owl of the Remove. 'Here comes Beaky – oh lor! Crikey!'

Down the hallowed corridors of Middle School indeed came Beaky; he of the protuberant proboscis and eagle eyes. The chaps of the Remove assumed a silence like unto the grave as the tyrannical professor swept through the door, his gown billowing behind him.

'Good morning, boys,' he boomed in a loud, hirsute voice as he peered at them from beneath his craggy stentorian brows.

'Good morning, sir,' answered the chaps of the Remove as Beaky stood at the window and looked out over the quad to the kipper-smoking factory, the coke ovens and the shunting yards.

'This afternoon, as you know only too well, is the annual sports day; all your paters and maters will be here' (cries of 'Oh lor!', 'Oh rot!', and 'Stinks!', 'Chizz!', 'Yah', 'Rather', etc) 'and we, that is the Doctor and myself, expect you to put up a good show, play the game, play up like men.' (Cries of 'Oh lor!' etc, many low moans.) 'The main event of the afternoon traditionally at the school has always been the cross-rubbish-tip, slum-clearance-site and back-entry run. This year the route will begin at the shunting yards, go down over the

39

tannery tip, along by the battery works and up Coke Street to the slag heaps. From there you'll leg out across the canal at the weir, cut round over the remains of Sebastopol Terrace and Inkerman Street, and down through the slaughter-yards. The last run is back over the canal near the brewery and round by the brass foundry and the gasworks near the cemetery. Is that clear?' (Low moans and mutters of 'Clear as mud', and 'Clear as a foggy day in a coal cellar'.)

'Good! In that case we'll continue with the un-rewarding but necessary practice of inculcating a little of the language of Ancient Rome into those rather thick crania of yours. Clegg Minor, you will construe from "And Aeneas set the prow of his boat towards the westering sun . . ." ' (Low mutters of 'How beastly', 'Boo', 'Stinks', 'Rotten egg', etc.)

That afternoon saw the famous five chums of the Remove perched in their running togs on the wall near the Dogs' Home at the back of the Corporation Wash House.

'Stinks to cross-rubbish-tip running, say I,' said Cherry.

'Double stinks,' said Clegg Minor.

'The stinkfulness is terrific,' said Ram Jam Full.

'Don you led de man give you no rass,' echoed Leroy Winston Jones.

'Oh lor, ouch, yarroo, groan!! I say, you chaps, I'm absolutely starving. I could eat a horse between two bread vans,' said the Fat Owl.

'Oh Fat Boy, the day you are not starving is the day that the Irish stop eating potatoes,' said Ram Jam Full, just to show that he could be as prejudiced as the best.

'I say,' said Cherry Arkwright, 'I've got a capital wheeze! Just for a jape let's duck out of the race near the glue-works and go to Ma Benson's for some tuck. We

40

can join up with the runners later and no one would be any the wiser.'

'What a wizard jape,' cried Clegg Minor.

'Wacko' and 'Yoiks!' cried the rest of the Famous Five, except Leroy Winston Jones who said, 'Dat's orlright 'cos I din' spek to do no runnin' anyway. I got a good piece of ganja I want to get me into.'

'Oh lor, ouch, yarooh,' uttered the Fat Owl as the rest of the Famous Five sat on him.

'Could you see your way towards financing the operation, Old Chum?' asked Clegg Minor.

'We saw the postal order you got at brekkers,' said Cherry.

'Oh lor, you rotters,' squealed the Fat Owl as the chums relieved him of the cash.

So the five chums punted over the wall and down Jubilee Street towards Ma Benson's tuck shop, the Fat Boy a few yards behind the rest, his goggles bobbing up and down as he lamented the loss of his five shilling postal order.

'I say, you beasts . . . oh lor . . . you stinkers.'

But all he heard before him was 'Good egg . . . Top hole' and 'The topfulness of the hole is terrific.'

Old Beaky stood on the edge of the gravel walk in his cricket flannels. Next to him was Emily, the Rector's daughter, on whom he was more than a little sweet. The afternoon sun glimmered palely through the smoke and smog as the paters and maters milled around the tea and sticky bun stall.

'They should be running up past the scrap-metal yard by now,' said Beaky, glancing at his watch. 'I say, I've got an idea! Why don't we stroll out a little and watch them coming along by the pork-scratching sheds, shall we?'

She nodded and gave him her demure arm and together they walked down Brunel Street. As they were passing Ma Benson's Tuck Shop Beaky heard the familiar tones of a voice that he knew only too well.

'I say, Ram Jam! Pass the pop will you?'

'Oh dear, dear, dear, the Fat Boy is having too much pop and is falling over.'

'That's Jam Full and Clegg Minor,' cried Beaky. 'Come along, my dear.' He pushed open the shop door only to find it empty. The voices he had heard had obviously come from the back of the shop. With a thunderous visage and Emily on his arm he strode purposefully and unasked around the counter full of gobstoppers and liquorice sticks, into Ma Benson's private quarters.

On the floor lay the Fat Boy, blind drunk. Leroy Winston Jones was lying beside him, the remains of a huge joint still dangling from the side of his mouth, while the rest of the Famous Five were evident only by their bottoms which were moving with enthusiastic regularity between the dimpled knees of Ma Benson and her two daughters.

'Oh lor, crikey! Crumbs, Hughie!!' moaned the Fat Boy, unable to rise.

'The crikeyfulness is terrific,' said Ram Jam Full, who had not the same problem.

'Will somebody tell me what is happening?' demanded Beaky, waxing his wroths.

'I'm broadening the boys' education, dearie,' shouted Ma Benson from beneath a breathless Clegg Minor. 'And you can have a glass of sarsaparilla and a humbug and wait your turn like a gentleman.'

Old School Tie

Roggers and I went to Eton together –
Fags and flogging and the Old School Tie,
Play the game, chaps, jolly boating weather,
Up school, up house, up everyone in sight.
Read Ovid in the Latin, Homer in the Greek,
Spankers' World three times a week.
Rah rah, sporting the Old School Tie
Rah rah, sporting the Old School Tie

Roggers and I were in the army together,
Roggers and I went through the Guards;
We both got cashiered together –
Thought a Bobby was a swaddy at Marble Arch.
Roggers and I want to bring flogging back
Just so long as we get a fair crack.

Rah rah, etc.

Roggers and I married two horsey sisters,
Buck-toothed ladies from the county set.
They've got faces like saddle blisters,
They can eat apples through a wire net.
Chinless wonders, we carry on the line–
Love those buck-teeth women with the nutcracker thighs.

Rah rah, etc.

Roggers he's well into rubber –
Wet suit on and flippers on his feet,
Covered all over in puncture patches,
Roggers flops round the Chelsea streets.
Roggers has trouble with his sex life
'Cos it's hard to find a frogman at twelve o'clock at night.

Rah rah, etc.

Roggers and I know Roddy and Bianca,
Roggers and I cross the world by jet,
Go to parties where there's wunches of bankers,
We're the darlings of the William Hickey set.
We set all the trends, wear the right clothes;
Tried sniffing coke but the bubbles went up me nose.

Rah rah, etc.

Roggers and I go shooting together
In the season at my country house.
With the gamekeeper's daughter I was in the heather;
He mistook my botty for a rising grouse –
Fourteen weeks I was lying in bed
With a mirror held behind me picking out lead.

The Unluckiest Man in the World woke up this morning and discovered he had been turned into Birmingham.

The Unluckiest Man in the World won a free holiday to Pontins, Krakatoa.

Sporting the Old School Tie

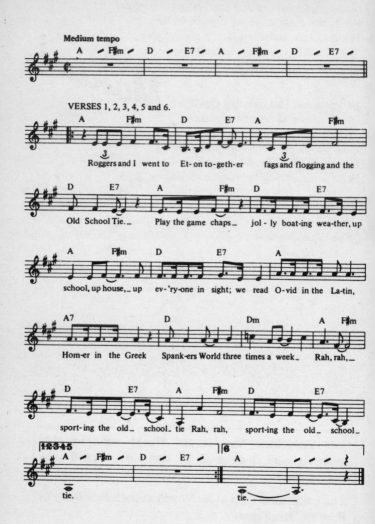

Manuel

Useful Spanish for the Innocent . . .

Eh hombre! que estes los aderezar cimento in mi casa pillocko?
What is this cement mixer doing in my room, my good friend?

El banjos es plenjos de muerdas.
The swimming pool is full of dead people.

Donde lata me puesto los dedo clavos recortes?
Where can I put these toenail clippings?

Sui es unas pelagroso slickos de doce kilometros Ambre Soleaire a la largo del costa.
There is a dangerous twelve kilometer Ambre Solaire slick along the coast.

Caricatura vosotros manos de mi esposa tetas/traseros/belsa.
Take your hands off my wife's breasts/buttocks/purse.

Ese no langoster, mi amigo, ese bacalao in carton!
This is not lobster, this is cod in cardboard!

Decira los chofos us unas chuckelos Inglesi.
Tell the chef it was an English joke.

Nosotros nevero tippos plenjos del dissos in Ingleterra.
We never tip more than this in England.

Eh mi amigo! Caramba! Attention! Que bustos majores!!!
Look, my friend, that young lady is charming.

Vosotros es unas grandes majores pillocko!
I wanted you to get rid of the cement mixer not bring another one, now there are two, young sir!

Basta!
Thank you!

AT THE BULLFIGHT . . .

Es como Old Traffordo con ajo!
It is like Old Trafford with garlic.

Porque los hombres ensayo poner los chaqueta sobre del vaca?
Why is he trying to put that jacket on the cow?

Los vaca parecerse tristos.
The cow looks unhappy.

Los toreador paracerse tristos.
The toreador looks unhappy.

Perque los toreador vamos?
Why is the toreador running?

Perque los toreador es sanguare?
Why is the toreador bleeding?

Los todos caricaturas della hospital?
Are they taking him off to hospital?

Los toreador es unas majores chiquitas blusa!
The toreador is a big girl's blouse!

50

Jo no comprenne sui es vosotros hermano!
I didn't know he was your brother!

Es un chuckelos Inglese, ha ha.
It was an English joke, ha ha.

Donde es los hospital proximo?
Where is the nearest hospital?

GENERAL SPANISH . . .

Vosotros esposa as unas facha como estampido del marranos traseros!!!
This is an Andalusian insult and should only be used in emergencies. Literally translated it means 'Your wife has a face like thunder from a pig's buttocks' and is usually followed with:
Es unas chuckelos Inglese, ha ha . . . donde es los hospital proximo?

The Unluckiest Man in the World found that his dog had got distemper and had decorated the ceiling.

The Unluckiest Man in the World tried to eat spaghetti with an electric drill and knitted himself a bed sock.

Manuel

Manuel worked in a chippy in Salford,
Manuel made the fat fly,
Till a loose-living lady called Gladly Gladys
On Manuel cast a glad eye.
Manuel took Gladys to the Ritz on a Friday,
Led her onto the floor
And as they danced, as they romanced,
The people all started to roar.

Chorus
'Cos Manuel danced the samba with no trousers on
And the people shouted 'Ole muchos cohon!!' (*Twice*)

Manuel's real name was Eric Winterbottom
Till he went on a package tour to Spain.
After two weeks on a Cook's tour in Ibetha
He came home and had his name changed.
All things Latin, they entranced him,
This pimply Salford youth,
He called his girlfriend Gladys, Yuanita,
'Cos she only had one tooth.

Manuel met Yuanita south of the border
Down Birmingham way,
She chewed terbacca and played the marraccas
In a sleazy Walsall café.
The moment he saw her, he fell for her
He knew where his heart lay.
Her flying marraccas made his eyes water
As she breathlessly whispered 'Ole!'

And Manuel and Yuanita travelled the country
Giving exhibition dances,
The Cha Cha, the Rhumba, Paso Doble and the Samba,
And Manuel danced with no pantses,
Till in a draughty Dance Hall in Dunfermline
Someone left a fridge door open wide
And a bitter cold blast caught Manuel as he spun past.
Two days later he died.

Gladys she pined for her Manuel,
Threw herself under a bus;
So they took her, in a grave they stuck her,
With the minimum of fuss.
Still they say down Salford way
At night when the gas-light flickers, Manuel he dances without
no pantses
And Gladys she dances also.

Manuel

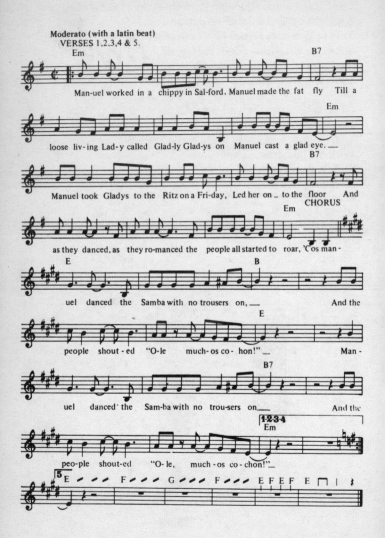

Moderato (with a latin beat)
VERSES 1,2,3,4 & 5.

Man-uel worked in a chippy in Sal-ford, Manuel made the fat fly Till a

loose liv-ing Lad-y called Glad-ly Glad-ys on Manuel cast a glad eye.

Manuel took Gladys to the Ritz on a Fri-day, Led her on _ to the floor And

CHORUS
as they danced, as they ro-manced the people all started to roar, 'Cos man-

uel danced the Samba with no trousers on, __ And the

people shout-ed "O-le much-os co - hon!" _ Man-

uel danced' the Sam-ba with no trou-sers on__ And the

1-2-3-4
peo-ple shout-ed "O-le, much-os co-cochn!"

5 E F G F EFEF E

For Carlo

Carlo always told us that the sauce he put on the ice cream he sold us was elephant's blood. Being only five or six years old at the time I imagined that he must go hunting elephants in his ice cream van and that being Italian he must naturally go back to Italy to do it. When I saw pictures of the Leaning Tower of Pisa in school it was obvious to me that the leaning was caused by the Italian wild elephants scratching their itchy sides on it. It's amazing how obvious all the puzzles of history become with the help of imagination.

The town clerk, Pisa, on the telephone . . .

'Hello, Dante? It's councillor Machiavelli here, 'ow are you, lad? 'Ow's that Beatrice of yours? Oh! I'm sorry to hear that, you seemed made for each other – anyhow, plenty more fish in t'sea, eh, lad? Any road up, what I've phoned about is t'tower – Aye, I think we've been done – I think that Irish subcontractor, Leonard O'Davinci, has skimped on t'foundations – Aye, it's leaning over like Boccaccio after a cecamaron – the whole town's out there laughing their nuts off at it . . . and yon Galileo's been up there all morning dropping cannon-balls and feathers off t'top to see which kills people the best . . . Never mind the bloody tourist attraction, *you* designed t'bloody thing . . . How are we going to explain all those expensive working lunches and the month's holiday in Carthage to get all t'plans sorted out? And the eight thousand ducats in the Florence and Bingley Building Society? I tell you, Dante, if this gets out there's some muck going to hit the fan – there's you, me, O'Davinci and Michaelangelo all in it up to our eyes – they're already after Michealangelo for the job he did on t'Vatican – t'Sistine chapel – aye, he used cheap pigments – an angel's head fell off the ceiling and killed

IS IT GETTING WORSE, OR AM I?

PISA BAR & RESTA

t'bloody Archbishop of Cremona last Lent, and the arms have fell off that Venus he did last month. If they find out about him watering down the distemper for the tower he'll be for t'marble quarries rest of us – look, we've got to do summat and fast!

'Aye! By 'eck, that's not a bad idea – sell t'tower to a family wi' one leg longer than the other – champion!! Aye, but you know what t'government are like about selling off council houses. Look, Dante owd lad, we're both masons, we're both in the same lodge, we know the score – I'm having tea with Borgias tonight – why don't we meet up at their place and talk about it there? Aye, about eight o'clock – see you there, then.'

The town clerk hangs up . . .

'Shame about Dante – he'll 'ave to go – he knows too much – I'll get Lucretia to make up one of her special puddings, put a little suicide note by his bed and – Roberto's your patron! – no one's the wiser. "Pressure of work", "guilty conscience", what 'ave you, plain as the nose on your face. Talking about that, I wonder how old Tycho Brahe's doing – haven't seen him for a bit – not since that fiddle with t'camera obscura, etc. etc . . .

The Unluckiest Man in the World found that he had caught termites off a lavatory seat.

For Carlo

Every Sunday in summer he came in his van,
The kids all shouted 'Here's Carlo, the ice cream man!'
Banging on doors as the van stopped and the bell rang,
And dads in armchairs woke up as the kids sang.

Chorus
Hey, Mam, give us some money for Carlo,
Hey, Mam, give us it quick before he goes.

He's raspberry sauce he tells us it's elephant's blood;
I don't think it is, but, Mam, it tastes real good.
He's wafers, cornets, ninety-niners and twists,
Oh, get your purse, Mam. Come on, Mam, get it quick.

Every year when the Whitsun procession came round
He'd walk with all the other Italians in town;
He carried the Madonna and gave us all a big smile
As the band played and the kids all cheered and went wild.

And now on summer Sundays I take my own kids
And we walk down that old street where I used to live.
I sit down in my Dad's old chair in the house,
The bell rings and the kids come in and all shout.

And they say . . .

'Hey, dad, give us some money for Carlo,
Hey, Dad, give us it quick before he goes,
Hey, Dad, hurry up, don't be so slow,
Hey, Dad . . .' All the kids they love Carlo.

For Carlo

The Upper Echelon

The Upper Echelon

Rodney's going out with Daphne,
Who was once engaged to Ted,
Till she found him lying naked
In her Mummy's double bed.
She wouldn't have minded him having Mummy,
But he was giving Daddy one instead –
God! It's brutal in the upper echelon.

And you remember that frightfully arty girl
Called Anne, but she called herself Olivia,
She married a retired Guards Officer
And ran a Gay Bar in Bolivia,
Well, she's got a divorce now
And a shop in Chelsea selling 'Fifties trivia –
We survive in the upper echelon.

Chorus
And I sometimes wonder, do the poor people do it like we do?
I always feel it should be reserved for the likes of me and you
Don't you?

I had to shoot my favourite hunter
At a meet in Chipping Beck,
'Cos he tripped over a dashed anti-blood sports creep
And fell and broke a leg.
So we took the rotter and thrashed him
Till we bleddy near broke his neck,
We love our animals in the upper echelon.

65

I met a working-class novelist
Last week at the Blemsby-Gores,
He picked his nose and farted and belched
And threw up on the parquet floor,
And I thought he was frightfully spiffing and earthy
When he called Mummy a capitalist whore –
We support the Arts in the upper echelon.

Chorus
My brother's trying to go gay
But he doesn't like it much,
So he's living with a lady brickie
Who's more than a little bit butch,
So we don't know who's doing what to whom
With what and for how much –
Sometimes it's confusing in the upper echelon.

When Mummy goes to the Bridge Club,
The gardener comes in for tea;
He's rather scruffy and smells of manure
But looks rather like Oliver Reed,
But he's built like an Arab donkey
And he goes like a sewing machine –
We know our onions in the Upper Echelon.

The Unluckiest Man in the World bought his wife a bunch of artificial flowers and they died.

The Upper Echelon

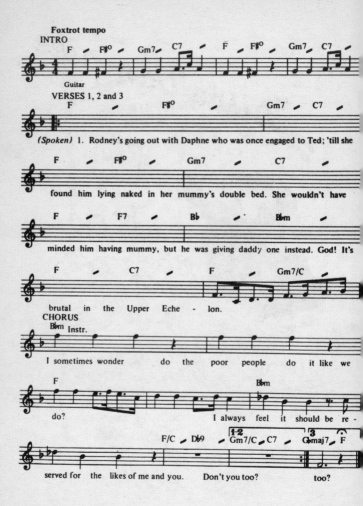

Foxtrot tempo
INTRO

Guitar

VERSES 1, 2 and 3

(Spoken) 1. Rodney's going out with Daphne who was once engaged to Ted; 'till she found him lying naked in her mummy's double bed. She wouldn't have minded him having mummy, but he was giving daddy one instead. God! It's brutal in the Upper Eche - lon.

CHORUS
Instr.

I sometimes wonder do the poor people do it like we do? I always feel it should be re-served for the likes of me and you. Don't you too? too?

Disco Vampire

The alarm clock rings, his half-asleep fingers fumble for the button and press it frantically, jabbing urgently in the pitch darkness. It is the wrong button. The Goblin Teasmade begins to pour boiling hot water in the dressing-table drawer. The bell is still ringing, sounding in his overhung brain like a thousand knights in suits of armour falling down an eternity of stone stairs in an empty castle. He stumbles through the darkness as steam fills the room, hopping on the freezing cold floor like a manic stork. Outside a bleak, black, before-dawn winter's morning. The bell is still ringing, screaming out like a million dried peas falling on a tin roof. He puts on his underpants. They are now the temperature of freshly brewed tea. Into the air he rises, screaming in pain, his wedding tackle the colour of an icelandic sunset.

The bell is still ringing. He kicks the Goblin Teasmade across the room, fusing the lights, and staggers round in the gloom clutching himself like a St Helen's forward about to make a try. He cracks his shins on the bed end and jumps back uttering profanities, only to split his head open on the wardrobe door. The bell is still ringing. Sobbing uncontrollably, a mere hairsbreadth from insanity, he brushes against the light cord over the bed end. Not realising that the lights are fused he pulls hard and repeatedly on the cord until a large portion of ceiling – complete with loft insulation and a pair of hibernating long-eared bats – descends under the influence of gravity to fill the room with plaster dust, distemper, several thousand polystyrene balls and a pair of disturbed and angry potential vampires.

His hand in the dark touches a shoe. He aims it at the flitting shapes in the gloom. His shoe hits the radio, switching it on. The alarm bell stops. It was next door's alarm clock.

'Hi there, morning people, you're listening to Radio Gibberdilly and this is Dodger Ray here. I'll be with you for the next seven hours – yes, folks! Seven whole hours! And I'll be playing you the hottest and newest sounds in disco. Taking us off on the launching pad is Ray's Tip For The Top – it's already number one and it's climbing fast – here it is, The Gooley Brothers and *I Love Birmingham* – here we go, babies – it's a spinneroolie from the Gooleys!!!!!'

The crazed voice is replaced instantly by a mechanical, metallic, pulsating rhythm over which a voice that sounds as though it has been modified as a result of a collision between a pair of tight trousers and a bicycle cross-bar croons 'Oooh Ooh, baby, Birmingham Crazy Disco I love it up I love it up' – all the arts and technology of two thousand years of man's progress from the caves and the mammoths distilled into one limping beat that sounds like a gang of rutting dust-carts, and a set of words that one monkey at one typewriter would have been bound to produce in less than half an hour. The record finishes and the gibberish starts again, its never-ending nonsense pounding into his brain.

He clings with his back to the wall – the bats are suspended in mid air. Like a wild beast or a thing possessed he slavers uncontrollably as Dodger Ray's Silly Phone In is contacted by four girls working in an American Ice Cream and Gooey Pancake parlour called Freezy Fred's. The gibberish doubles in intensity as

Dodger Ray and the girls talk for aeons about how bad the line is and which discos they go to and which records they like. On the turntable, spewing out over the airwaves, goes another piece of musical wallpaper indistinguishable from the other called *Mutant Disco* by Duncan Disorderly . . .

> 'Even mutants got to dance
> Give us three-legged dancers a chance
> Oh Mutant Disco
> Rotate, mutate, all the sounds are great
> I've got three legs, she's got eight
> At the ooooh oooh oooh she bap
> Ooooooh ooooh ooooh disco.'

For four hours, unable to move, he clings to the wall, his brain cells begging for mercy. Then, unable to stop himself, he flees from the room in his underpants. His eyes glazed, he leaps into his car and drives like an automaton through the slowly lightening streets until he comes to downtown Radio Giberdilly. He pushes past the commissionaire.

'Have you come for a car sticker or a Radio Gibberdilly teeshirt?' asks the girl on reception.

'GNAAR! SMARG! KRAAAAAZGMORGSPLOOT!' he screams. She faints. He lurches along the corridors, foam flecks wisping from the corners of his cracked lips, until he hears the voice he is seeking.

'Don't forget, people, write into Radio Gibberdilly and we'll send you a free aerosol can of Doggy Poo remover. You know, I was talking to a woman yesterday and she said "Hello" and I said "Hello!" back. Isn't that absolutely fantastic, people? I want you to phone into our Very Boring Half Hour and tell me if something just as fantastic has happened to you anyway here's a record for all of you going to Spain for your hols . . .'

But before he can utter another gibber, Norman Normal – he of the casseroled balls – has committed radio's first live murder. It isn't long before all the other radio stations find this a great way of increasing audience numbers and soon regular snuff shows became a part of everyday broadcasting until the average lifespan of a disc jockey from training to death is seventeen hours.
A further note.

On the day that Norman Normal acted on behalf of mankind record shops were besieged by people taking back their copies of Costa Del Disco because it hadn't got all the gurgles, chokes and whimpers on it.

The Unluckiest Man in the World bought a sun-dial and found that it was slow.

The Unluckiest Man in the World was so unlucky a black cat crossed his path and killed him. It was a panther.

Disco Vampire

The word is goin' round
All over the town,
Because of all them disco dancers
Keep fallin' down.
They take them to the city morgue,
Then they do a check,
Find that all the stiffs
Got holes in the neck.

Chorus
He's a disco . . . vampire,
He's a disco . . . vampire,
He's a disco . . . vampire,
He's a raver from the grave.

He drives a big flash car
An E type jugular –
And drinks a Bloody Mary
Standing at the disco bar,
Like an ordinary bloke,
With his cane and his black cloak –
No one knows he's there
Till people start to croak.

Blood is thicker than water
To this Transylvanian Travolta;
If you let him near your girlfriend
She's sure to end up altered.
He lays a load of booze on
And gets them in confusion
And while they're dancing cheek to cheek
He has a quick transfusion.

He's the champ of all the vamps
In the flashin' disco lamps;
If you're wearing garlic
His style will be cramped,
So if you're dancing with a batman
And his dentures don't fit –
Don't be sucker's supper,
It's time for you to split.

The Unluckiest Man in the World found a bunch of bananas but they were all empty. The tree had had wind.

The Unluckiest Man in the World won a record of Bernard Manning singing *Tubular Bells*.

The Unluckiest Man in the World spent all his life savings to build a swimming pool and it burned down.

The Unluckiest Man in the World got savaged by a killer tortoise.

Disco Vampire

Chain Store
Father Christmas

'Magic Cave Control to Sledge Five . . . peep peep . . . this is Magic Cave Control to Sledge Five . . . come in, Sledge Five.'

'Sledge Five here, come in, Magic Cave Control.'

'We've just had a Yuletide Yuletide* from Sledge Six over in Birmingham, claims he's had a close encounter of the second kind, Sledge Five, claims he's seen flashing saucer-shaped humming objects over the Bullring.'

'He's pissed again, Magic Cave Control . . . it's the same as last year . . . he's never content with the glass of milk and the mince pies, he's got to sniff out the cooking sherry and the brandy and cigars and the chocolate liqueurs. Last year he got so smashed he ran into the back of another reindeer team. Took two days to sort them all out, dogs were running out throwing buckets of water on them . . . it was murder.'

'OK, Sledge Five . . . but keep your eyes open all the same.'

'Wenceslas . . . Magic Cave Control.'

'Wenceslas, Sledge Five.'

Sledge Five carried on making his drops; a pram here, a bike there, a junior poisoner's outfit here, twenty-seven white golliwogs in Bermondsey. Sledge Five was just knocking off for a tea break when over the roof-tops came a strange saucer-shaped object. Glowing, myster-

* Mayday Mayday

81

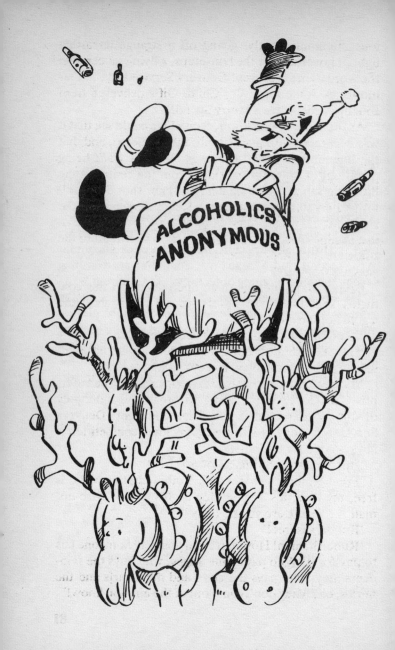

ious, humming gently, giving off a strange unearthly light, it hovered over the housetops, a flying saucer with the words 'Ersatz Present Delivery Service Ltd . . . Our motto: A Smile for Every Child. Gifts delivered from £50. upwards. Have a Merry Spend!!!'

As the saucer came lower, Santa Five could see that it was decorated with plastic holly and mistletoe, and that the humming he could hear was *Deck the Halls* being piped out of holes on the side. From the centre of the hovering saucer a glaring beam of light shot down followed by a shining ramp that led from the saucer to the roof-tops. Down the ramp came a man-like creature clad in a shining silver suit. Embroidered on the breast of the suit were the words BRUCEY BABY . . . BRUCEY'S THE NAME – PRESSIES THE GAME.

Brucey Baby had his tunic open (even on this cold night), split down to his navel to reveal a hairy chest and a gold bullion medallion.

'Ciao!!' he said, waving his hand in greeting.

'Hey, Gobshite! What's all this delivery service nonsense?' asked Santa Five, more than a little angry.

'It's free enterprise, baby, that's what it is, free enterprise, my love. We're going to break the monopoly of the nationalized Santa Claus Present Delivery Service . . . Look at it this way, my love, competition is always good for business.'

'But ours isn't a business, ours is free!'

'Free! Nothing's free, baby. Nothing in this world is free, my love, it's dog eat dog in this world. Wise up, man . . . Where are you at, baby?'

'But ours is free!'

'Rubbish, man! How naïve can you get? Someone has to pay for it! Who pays your wages, who buys the reindeers' hay, who pays the elves and the dwarfs and the fairies, eh? They don't come out of the air, you know!'

83

'Santa Claus Number One sorts it all out!'

'OK, and where does he get the bread from? Wise up, man, everybody's on the make nowadays. You bet that Santa's got some sort of a fiddle going, sweet. Everybody's got a fiddle going.'

'But we're real!' exclaimed one of the many real Father Christmasses.

'Bollocks,' said the Ersatz Delivery man, who was just about to climb in the chimney when Real Father Christmas Number Five fetched him a swift boot up the Fiorucci pants that sent him arse over tip off the roof amongst the snowy dustbins far below.

'Merry Christmas,' he chuckled as he took the reins again and sent Sledge Number Five soaring off into the frosty night.

The Unluckiest Man in the World overslept on the Day of Judgement and found that they'd pulled the ladder up.

Chain Store Father Christmas

I'm a chain store Father Christmas,
By me bran tub here I sit,
A million kids have graced me knees,
I've done me Christmas bit.
'Ho Ho Ho! How Jolly Hi Ham!'
I know all my lines;
The only trouble is –
I hate the little swines.

They come in here with sticky fingers,
Rub them everywhere,
Put chewing gum in me whiskers
And toffees in me hair.
They're either running round amuk
Or else they're scared to death,
And they scratch and bite and kick you
And widdle down your legs.

They ask 'How does a man as fat
As you get down our chimney?'
And 'I want a nuvver pressie from the tub
And not that rubbish you give me!'
And one kid grabbed me by the throat
And shouted in me ear,
'Don't make a cobblers of it this time
Like you did last year.'

One kid hit me fairy help –
His wings are all in shreds,
And his wand got bent when one kid hit
Him with it on the head.
The dwarfs were in the pub all day
And came in here risotto,
Staggering round and falling down
Blotto in me grotto.

The elves and gnomes are all on strike,
The fairies all in tears,
The polar bear has got the sulks
And Noddy's bashed Big Ears.
The Goblin King has lost his throne,
The reindeers' antlers are broke,
A kid dropped his fag in me bran tub
And me baubles went up in smoke.

So I sit here in me grotto,
I've got the Yuletide blues.
Some kids have smashed the Goblin King,
The dwarfs are on the booze;
Me trouser legs are soaking wet,
I've chewing gum in my whiskers;
I'm supposed to be all jolly and merry –
But I hate Christmas.

The Unluckiest Man in the World was trapped in a car for four hours with Tony Blackburn on the radio.

Chain Store Father Christmas

Akroyd's Funeral

It was dark as a coal-hole picnic
On the day Grandad Akroyd dropped dead;
Work was scarce as rocking-horse droppings,
Not a church roof for miles had lead.

So cold that the flame on the candle
Got frozen one Wednesday night,
And we had to warm it up in the oven
Before we could get it to light.

Some brass monkeys outside sung carols soprano
You could 'ear 'em cursin' and swearin',
As they wandered round lost in the cold and the frost
They couldn't find their bearings.

On Sunday our chicken for dinner
Was a pigeon from off next door's loft
And me Dad pumped it up with his bike pump too hard
And our Sunday dinner buggered off.

'What would you like to eat now, Dad?'
Said our Mam, picking her nose,
'Hard boiled eggs,' our Dad said,
'You can't get your fingers in those.'

We couldn't afford to kill the chicken
So we boiled some water up hot,
And with bunches of dried peas tied to its knees
It paddled about on the top.

Me Grandad had mortgaged his pension till 1994,
While me Gran in her vest
Was outside doing her best
With a red light above t'coal shed door.

'I can't stand't no more,' the old man cried,
A mad light shone in his glass eye,
'We'll have to defraud the insurance man –
Hands up, I want a volunteer to die.'

Mam said she would have, but she were too busy,
Our Albert said his library book was due back,
Gran said she would but her and her mate
Had got tickets for last Saturday's match.

So we drew straws to settle the matter,
But there was never no doubt
'Cos me Dad cut me Grandad's in half wi't' bread-knife,
Just as he was pulling it out.

'I'm too old to die,' he said, using the cat
As a club to belabour me Dad,
'All right,' me Dad says, 'you don't have to die –
Just lie down and pretend as you are.'

So me Grandad lay down on the hearth-rug,
And we called the doctor in.
Me Gran took out a bottle and glasses
And got him smashed on her dandelion gin.

He said me Grandad had died of a very rare disease,
A bad case of tropical frost-bite,
Then he staggered off out and we all heard a shout
From the street 'cos he slipped in some dog shite.

Our Billy ran round for the man from the Pru,
Gran filled him with dandelion gin,
He paid £4.10 in used chip shop yen
And said, 'When are you burying him?'

'Oh, we weren't thinking of burying him,' Grandma said,
'Thinking of having him stuffed meself,
Or embalming him in that Plasticraft
And keeping him on't mantelshelf.'

'Nay, yon is illegal,' said Man from Pru.
'Grandad will have to be buried
In a box and shroud in constipated ground.'
At this Grandad looked reet worried.

Man from the Pru said he'd come to the burying
And see as how things were done quite right,
Then he staggered off out and we all heard a shout
From the street 'cos he slipped on that stuff that I told you
    about before.

'I've just done that,' said the doctor,
So the insurance man rubbed his nose in it.

So the pretend corpse now had to be buried,
Me Dad got an old kipper crate,
When the holes got plugged and the wood it looked good
With plastic brass handles on – great.

'We'll only bury you just till he's gone,
Then we'll dig you up, honest,' Dad said.
Took a bottle of gin before Grandad gave in
And lay int' box to play dead.

Me Gran looked down at the box saying 'What a lovely corpse,'
Tears fell on her dripping and toast,
When the body at rest shoved his hand up her vest, saying
'Now then, how's that for a ghost?'

So we put the box on big Mabel's coal cart
And off to t'cemetery we set,
We followed on bikes and all seemed quite right
Until another burying we met.

A policeman was stood on point duty,
'Cos there was a fault on the traffic lights,
But he fell to the ground with his arms flaying round
'Cos he slipped on the road on another load of all that stuff I
    was telling you about before.

'We just done that,' said the doctor and the insurance man,
So the policeman rubbed their noses in it.

As he spun on the ground the traffic flew round,
And the two buryings got in a jam,
Their driver took a poke at me Dad wi' a wrench
And got a kick up the shoemaker's off me Mam.

When we sorted it out we'd got the wrong box;
Grandma said, 'Ee, we won't see no more of him,'
When their driver come round our burying we found
Had gone to the crematorium.

By the time that we got there the service was done,
You could hear the organ play
As the congregation wept hankies and sniffed,
And our kipper box was on its way.

The shutters were open, we all heard the flames,
And suddenly Grandad gave a yell,
And a coffin with legs and its arse end on fire
Ran out on t'conveyor belt!

Over the pews and out through the window,
The burning kipper box ran,
And we all cheered the crate as it swam through the lake
Chased by me Dad and me Mam.

'A blessed miracle,' said me Gran,
But the Man from the Pru went quite white;
'Ruined,' he roared, he would have said more
But he slipped in the road on some more of that stuff I've been
    telling you about.

'I've just done that,' said the policeman,
So the insurance man rubbed his nose in it.

The Unluckiest Man in the World wore a lucky rabbit's foot all the time and became the first recorded case of myxomatosis in human beings.

The Unluckiest Man in the World bought a rocking-horse for Christmas and it died on Boxing Day.

The Unluckiest Man in the World went fishing and caught an old boot but it got away.

Ladies' Man

He was a ladies' man (wah wah),
A real Don Juan (wah wah),
Lurking round all the bars and bistros,
All of the dance halls, the café and discos,
Pulling wives and spinsters,
Sisters and widows,
And even the occasional gran.

From nine to five
To keep himself alive
He worked in the Co-op, slicing bacon,
Sending the ladies home, hearts aching,
With nostrils flared and pupils dilating
At the way he fingered their pork.

Chorus
With his brylcreamed hair and mohair suit,
His cigarette-holder and his brown suede shoes,
Like the fox that got into the chicken coop
He was a ladies' man.

He was a married man –
Perfidious Don Juan;
When his wife got ready for the Weight Watchers' Club,
He told her he was playing darts at the pub.
He kept his Don Juan suit in an old wooden tub
And got changed in the garden shed.

Seven nights a week
This Scunthorpe sheikh
Oiled his toupee and trimmed his tash,
Garden-rollered his suit till it looked dead flash,
And knowing he was going out on the mash,
He made sure he'd got his packet of three.

Chorus
At the Tropicana
He met a lass called Anna.
With his billiard chalk behind his ear
He fixed his face in a seductive leer,
Bought her a bag of scratchin's and a half of beer,
Some crisps and a pickled egg.

All through the night
He held her tight,
Thigh to thigh in the Bossa Nova;
He pressed his suit did this Casanova,
With breathy sighs he swore he'd love her
If she'd come for a walk outside.

Chorus
In the Corporation park
Near the bowls' hut in the dark,
He nibbled her ear and kissed her lips,
Tickled her thighs and stroked her hips
And reached for his packet of three.

He opened her dress,
Slid his hand inside her vest –
But what he found was a real shocker!
'Cos instead of a soft warm pair of knockers
Was the hairy chest of a very gay docker
Who'd shaved just an hour before.

He turned and ran
This confused man,
But before he'd reached the pitch and put
He was grabbed at the back of the parkie's hut
And without benefit of clergy or an if or a but,
He became a mans' man as well.

Chorus
Now this ladies' man,
One-time Don Juan,
Stays in knitting by the fire at night,
Away from dance halls and bright city lights
And women with hairs curling out through their tights
And a bad case of barber's rash.

Last chorus
No more brylcreamed hair or mohair suit,
No more cigarette-holder or brown suede shoes,
Like a fox that met a bulldog in a chicken coop
He once was a ladies' man.

Ladies' Man

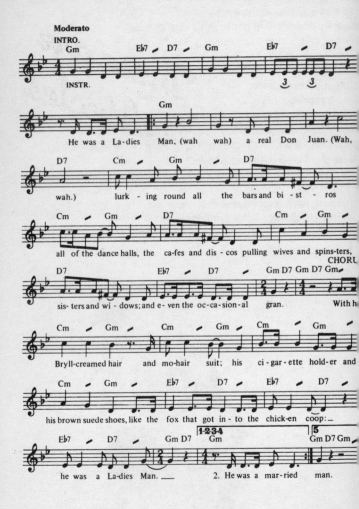

Moderato

INTRO.

INSTR.

He was a La-dies Man, (wah wah) a real Don Juan. (Wah, wah.) lurk - ing round all the bars and bi - st - ros all of the dance halls, the ca-fes and dis-cos pulling wives and spins-ters, sis - ters and wi - dows; and e - ven the oc-ca-sion-al gran.

CHORUS

With hi

Bryll-creamed hair and mo-hair suit; his ci - gar - ette hold-er and his brown suede shoes, like the fox that got in - to the chick-en coop:—

he was a La-dies Man. ___ 2. He was a mar-ried man.

These are
My Uncles

There should be a law that allows you to choose your own relatives, but there isn't – in my opinion this is a dire oversight on the part of the Almighty or someone. Some thoughts at random on relatives . . .

You can usually sort out who you want to marry yourself; when it comes to other important relationships, however, you find yourself lumped with all sorts of loonies, fascists, Tories, child molesters and murderers under the guise of 'family'. Almost everybody has uncles who get drunk and tell boring stories, or have bad breath/feet and dandruff and moult over people, or play the saxophone at three o'clock in the morning, or eat crackers over your record player, or use your best knives as screwdrivers or crowbars, or borrow your favourite book and when you get it back they've been using a rasher of bacon as a bookmark. Everybody has a distant cousin who uses the bathroom and always forgets to flush the toilet, leaving huge indestructible George the Thirds that refuse to go away for weeks or even months.

Relatives have been the death of some people, e.g. Cain, Nero, Crippen, Lizzie Borden.

There is no law which says you have to love your relations. Some people probably hate most of their nearest and dearest. The cousins of Ghenghis Khan probably detested him. You can imagine the scene in Ghenghis' yert on the Steppes:

'Aunty Mattila, your Ghenghis just ate all my soldiers!'

'Don't be such a softy, Tamburlaine. Aunty will make some more for you to dip in your egg.'

'But these were real soldiers, Aunty!'

FACT 1: Most murdered people are related to the people who murdered them.

FACT 2: Most murders are committed on a Monday.

CONCLUSION: Stay away from relatives on Monday.

FACT 3: More people are in mental institutions because of pressures within the family than any one other reason.

e.g. *The Family Reunion* by T. H. Eliot (the chocolate coloured poet)

ACT ONE – Scene One

An English family seat in the 1930s.

All the action takes place in the front room, which is furnished in the style of the period, very lavishly and very expensively. The actors are sitting round the room in easy chairs. On all the walls are hunting trophies ranging from the head of an elephant down to the head of a rat. The rugs and seat covers are made from animal skins and all have the heads still attached. There are six people in the room, all of whom look like animals. In the centre of the room a Chippendale table is blazing away. Everybody ignores it.

ELIZABETH He'll be here soon.

MARY We're all mad.

JEAN Sound without meaning, noise without fury, voice without sound – we are the dry crackles of leaves in an empty forest – we are molluscs clinging to a rock in a still pool.

RODNEY	(*talking to the rat's head on his hands and knees*) 'Course, she's off her jolly old chump, you know – quite nutty the whole bloody lot of them are off their crusts. There's only you and me right round here, and I'm not too sure about you. You don't say much but you're always bloody well grinning. Still, they say 'still waters run deep', eh?
SIMEON	Light without darkness – sense without feeling – tomorrow is yesterday and today is yellow – the clock in the hall has gone for a walk.
RODNEY	That's another one off his friggin' rocker – they're all bloody batty! Load of loonies.
ELIZABETH	He'll be here soon, he said he'd leave the station at eleven o'clock and it's Wednesday now – he said Monday but his watch doesn't always work.
MARY	Would you like some tea?
ELIZABETH	Yes, please. (*Mary pours the tea over Elizabeth*) Oh, you forgot the sugar! I hate tea without sugar! (*Mary empties the sugar bowl on her head*) Thank you.
RODNEY	Who the hell's she talking about? Who's coming? We're all here, for God's sake!
MARY	Edward, of course – he's coming to make everything complete.
RODNEY	Oh, Edward (*to the rat*), he's bloody crackers too – he's probably the worst of the lot.
NORMAN	I had a bike once, it didn't eat much, but my mother wouldn't let me keep it in the house. One frosty night it died.
JEAN	We are dry sticks rattling in the wind – we are the eye of a needle – we are the tongue of a hurricane.

NORMAN Is that an anagram? Hurricane (*thinks*) – I know – charabanc!
 (*Enter Edward*)

EDWARD Hello, everybody, sorry I'm late, I've been followed all the way by an iceberg and a Gurkha regiment playing kazoos. The iceberg wasn't playing kazoos, of course, it was the Gurkhas. Funny thing, language, isn't it? Do we mean what we mean or say what we think we say?

ALL An iceberg?
 (*Enter an iceberg*)

ALL But where are the Gurkhas?

EDWARD I made them up.

RODNEY I told you he was bloody crackers.
 (*Exeunt omnes*)

The Unluckiest Man in the World took a packet of Polos to Lourdes and the holes healed up.

These are My Uncles

Poor Uncle Albert,
He really can't help it,
For his only desire
Is the boys in the choir;
He's a sick vicar but those boys they are quicker
Than him, that's no sin
All through the graves and the naves he raves,
Puffin' and pantin', after matins.

Chorus
These are my uncles,
My skin and bones and flesh and blood and carbuncles.
(*Twice*)

Poor Uncle Mike,
His wife she was the village bike;
For a bottle of cider
Anyone could ride her –
Sailors and whalers from Mumps to Venezuela
All had tried and had a ride.
She'd handlebars and pedals, souvenirs and medals,
And a bell, lights as well.

Poor Uncle Fred
Was a demon in bed –
Or so people said –
But his pencil had no lead.
One night in the dark behind the bandstand in the park,
He goosed a statue of Stanley Matthews,
'Cos poor uncle Fred in his pencil has some lead –
But what could he do, no one to write to.

Poor Uncle Harry,
Things fall off lorries
Under his feet
As he walks down the street –
Cameras and suits, radios and boots,
He finds them all, when they fall,
Yet somehow they manage never to get damaged
In the fall, a miracle.

Poor Uncle Dan
Is a most peculiar man –
Ladies' undies on lines,
He steals them all the time.
In tights and brassieres Dan will career
Up and down, round the town,
He never gets arrested whenever he's detected
'Cos he is . . . the chief inspector.

These are My Uncles

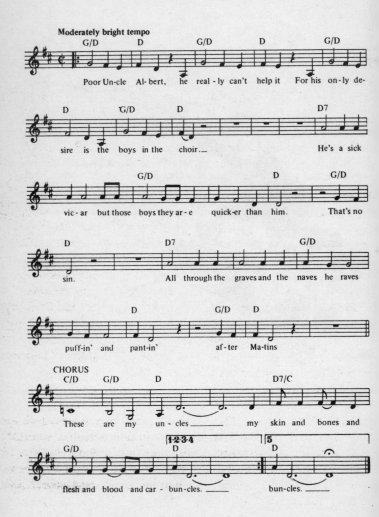

P.S. God

GOD U.K. Inc. Holdings Ltd – a play

Characters in order of appearance
God, God's Secretary, Mrs Nora God, God Junior, Archangel Fred, Satan, Satan's Manager. All the characters are Americans except Satan, who is Russian or Chinese.

(In the Dury Lane production Margaret Thatcher played all the God family)

ACT ONE – Scene One

A cloud with a desk and chair on it. Behind the desk a wall chart with a sales graph on it and the legend PARADISE PROMOTIONS WORLDWIDE. Hanging in the air by a miracle is the motto YOU DON'T HAVE TO BE MAD TO WORK HERE BUT IT HELPS written in poker work on a piece of wood with 'A present from Morecambe' on it. On the desk is a sign saying I MAY BE WRONG BUT I'M STILL RIGHT . . . GOD. On another cloud is a ticker tape machine ticking away.

God is sat at his desk wearing a suit with a carnation in the lapel and a pair of hornrimmed glasses. His hair is thinning and he is reading the Financial Times. *The two facts are not unconnected. Occasionally he uses an electronic calculator and mutters to himself.*

Enter God's Secretary, floating.

SECRETARY   Good morning Big G. I've just got the Christianity figures in for 1977-78. Here's the Rome Report, it only goes up to the last quarter. Unfortunately, it includes the Lent offerings so we're a bit down on the Christmas quarter. The St Joseph's Penny helped a bit but the foreign missions are well down on last year; people aren't into lepers any more. Oh and look here (*pointing*), the Methodists have sent their report in and they are well below par. The trouble with Methodists is they don't drink. People who don't drink don't throw money in collecting boxes as readily as those who do.

GOD   (*looking up from the report*) Haven't these Methodists ever read St Paul? 'Take a little wine for thy stomach's sake,' he says, '*take*' a little wine . . . it doesn't say 'please' or 'will you?' or 'would you like?' it says 'TAKE', God damn it! What's the use in me employing good writers like Paul if they don't take any notice of what he writes? He don't come cheap, that Paul, you know . . . he charges by the word not by the Epistle!

SECRETARY   Well, it looks as though we're going to have trouble there . . . we may even have to wind up that side of the business . . . the Jehovah's Witnesses are in trouble as well – the last recruiting drive they had they all ended up with septic knuckles and postman's leg.

GOD   These figures are terrible. What's the latest membership report like?

SECRETARY   Not so good – the last soul-count was terrible.

GOD   (*putting down his cigar and staring into the
             middle distance*) Perhaps we need another
             disaster, another Flood; or perhaps a
             plague of frogs, eight million de Gaulles;
             what about another Hiroshima, hey? Fig-
             ures went up after Hiroshima; plenty of
             Hiroshimas in the stock cupboard.

SECRETARY   I don't think it's that that we need, although
             the vengeful God bit always impressed the
             Jews. All that fire and brimstone bit might
             get a bit more money out of them. But the
             Christians have become more temporal,
             somehow – more earthly. Latest behavioral
             figures show that more people clean their
             cars on a Sunday than go to church.

GOD   No shit – you gotta be joking!

SECRETARY   More people watch *Stars on Sunday* than go
             to church in the whole of Europe.

GOD   Hey! What is all this? Don't give me this
             crap! We've got the biggest soul saving off
             planet insurance investment company in
             the universe. What about our sales cam-
             paigns: 'Go with God' – 'Pie in the Sky
             When You Die' – the 'Pick Your Own
             Cloud Unreal Estate Development Cor-
             poration' – 'Paradise Premium Bonds'?
             What about Billy Graham, Luther, Calvin,
             The Exorcist? Quo Vadis? The Robe? Why
             aren't they all on their knees in the churches
             mumbling 'Save me, save me!' Jesus! (*He
             paces the cloud*) What do the market re-
             search people say?

SECRETARY   Well, well, it's . . .

GOD   Don't 'well, well, well'! Fink! I want facts
             and I want them now!

SECRETARY	Well, the P.R. people say . . . it's your image.
GOD	(*shouting*) Image!
SECRETARY	Don't shout, they'll think it's thunder down below.
GOD	OK, OK, let me calm down . . . where's my tablets? I forgot, I gave them to Moses. OK, OK. What do you mean, 'Image'?
SECRETARY	Well, down there it's still the long white nightie, the long grey hair, the long white beard, the kindly face . . .
GOD	What, they're still using those William Blake P.R. handouts?
SECRETARY	We thought the historical approach was –
GOD	You dumb asshole, that went out with fish on Fridays. Get me a call – long distance – the Vatican. (*Picks up the phone when he's through*) Hello, Pope . . . who'm I speaking to? No, I want the Pope . . . Pope Goesthaveazel, that's right. Ah hello, Pope, Big G. here – the family is fine – and yours? Great, great, look we got to do somethin' about the Image, OK? Not yours, yours is fine, love it, love it, the hat, the curly pole, waving from the balcony, everything. No, we got to work on my image . . . got to update it a little. I want you to take down all the statues and the pictures – the whole works – I'm having a new set done with the suit, the hornrimmed glasses, the hand-made shoes, the lot . . . corporate image and likeness . . . that's it, just like the Masons, like the Mafia, good boy! You got the idea!

P.S. God

I don't want to sound
Silly, dear God,
But I been thinkin' very hard
'Cos my teacher said
You made all the world
And even bits of our back yard,
But I want to know, do you get dressed up
On a Sunday and go walkin' out
In itchy clothes and squeaky shoes,
An' if you gerrum mucked up, does the Holy Ghost shout,
Give you a clout?

I don't want to sound
Daft, dear God,
But I been thinkin' quite a lot
Ever since I pinched
A penny chew
From the counter at the corner shop.
My teacher said that pinchers go to hell
An' if that's true then I'm sure
If I'd known then I were goin' down there
I'd a pinched a bloomin' sight more than a penny chew –
I would 'ave 'ad two, or nine, or a few . . .

I don't want to sound
Like a big girl's blouse,
But if you're all that good
Why don't you stop
Them big ones at school
From bashin us likkle ones up?
Big MulQueen with his knuckly hands
Keeps twistin' me arm till I cry,
So if you won't hit 'im wiv a thunderbolt
Then make me twice his size, I'll give him two black eyes,
Make 'im eat snot pies.

Well, I don't want to sound
Stupid, God,
In this letter I'm sending' you,
But does your mam
Make you eat your cabbage
Like my mam makes me do?
I fink cabbage tastes like snot
And I don't like cabbage an' peas.
Why did you 'ave to invent that muck
When you could've made ice cream grow on trees,
Stead o'dem peas.

Well, that's really
All, dear God,
But P.S. just a minute,
Last Christmas Day I got a cracker,
I got a cracker,
And it 'ad nuffin' in it.
All the ovver kids got blowers and fings
And they were lettin' um off.
I don't want to spoil your birfday
But I fink Santa Clause is rippin' you off,
Him an' 'is elves, 'elpin demselves.

The Unluckiest Man in the World started school as a child and when his mother gave him his dinner money he ate it.

P.S. God

Moderato

VERSES 1,2,3,4 & 5.

don't want to sound ___ sil - ly dear God, but I've been think-in' ___ ve -ry

hard. 'Cos my teach - er said you made all the world, ___ and

ev - en bits of our ___ back yard. But I want to know do you

get dressed up on a Sunday and go walk-in' out in itch- y clothes and

squeaky shoes. An' if you ger - rem mucked up does the Hol-y Ghost

shout, give you a clout. ___ ___ 'elp-ing them - selves.

The Man' 'Nited Song

Me, I support Man' 'Nited
Wherever the team goes,
Wearin' me Doc Martin's
An' scruffy tatty clothes.
We're the Doc's Red Army,
We'll support 'im evermore,
'Cos we like kickin' 'eads in
An' rollin' about on the floor.

2, 4, 6, 9 'oo de we apprecimate
M.A.N. U.N.I.T.E.D.
Nut boot wallop and run,
Faces full of dandruff,
We never watch the match,
We're too busy 'avin' fun.

We go to all the foreign games
To bash some foreign 'eads in,
Kickin' all the wogs
Is lots and lots of fun.
We always smash in foreigners,
'Specially if they're lippy!
'Cos in the war, me dad said,
They come and they bombed our chippy.

We get dead excited
When the kick-off whistle goes,
Stickin' in the 'ead bit
And exchangin' nuts an' blows.
We never 'ave bin beaten,
We're always victoriyus,
'Specially if there's one of them
An' ninety-seven million of us.

I got a bird what comes wiv me
To all the 'Nited matches,
Steel toecaps in 'er tights
An' 'alf bricks in 'er bra;
We're gonna get us married
Soon as she gets out of prison
An' gonner 'ave lots and lots and lots
Of baby 'ooligans . . .

Me social worker says
I've got council estate paranoia;
Me probation officer wants me
To scrub old people's steps;
But I just like stickin' the 'ead
In other teams' supporters
An' pullin' the arm off me teddy bear
'Cos I'm one of the loyal reds.

The Unluckiest Man in the World met a fairy who granted him three wishes provided he made them on 30 February.

The Unluckiest Man in the World got an Easter egg for a Christmas present.

The Unluckiest Man in the World tried to kill himself by taking an overdose of scrabble tiles and ended up word-bound.

The Man' 'Nited Song

Can't Help Lookin' on the Bright Side

Over-optimism has been the death of many a man. Some over-optimistic quotes from history:

'Hey, Harold, look at all those geese in the sky coming towards us! Oh, they're not geese!' – Hastings, 1066

'How was I to know it was an albatross?' – Unknown deckhand aboard the Titanic, 14 April 1912

'It's alright, the tribes round here are friendly.' – General Custer

'My Adolph's a good boy!' – Mrs Hitler

'If the waters parted long enough for the Israelites to get through we'll have no problem.' – The dead captain of a lot of drowned Egyptians

---

The Unluckiest Man in the World bought a goldfish and it drowned.

I've got piles, each time I smile
My smiles they drive my piles wild,
But I can't help smiling once in a while
'Cos I can't help lookin' on the bright side.

My wife ran off with the bloke next door;
I never cursed, I never swore,
The poor bugger's got my mother-in-law –
You can't help lookin' on the bright side.

Chorus
'Cos it's true,
There's always someone worse off than you.
It's only chance –
You could have rheumatics and St Vitus' Dance.
Vodio vodio wah wah
Vodio vodio wah wah
Vodio vodio vodio do
Vodio vodio day.

Workin' on a buildin' site, tumbled off a wall,
Fell fifty foot – wasn't hurt at all
'Cos I landed on the foreman and he broke my fall –
You can't help lookin' on the bright side.

Bought a watch for a whole week's pay,
Broke it goin' home but I wasn't dismayed
'Cos it's still fairly accurate twice a day –
You can't help lookin' on the bright side.

Chorus
I went to the doctor's with a bit of a cough,
He said 'Stand there, take all your clothes off.'
When I asked him why, he said 'I like a good laugh –
And I can't help lookin' on the bright side.'

Money's shrinkin' but the bills are growin',
The rent for ma corporation tent's still owin',
It's bein' so cheerful keeps me goin' –
I can't help lookin' on the bright side.

Chorus
Got no money and I've got no wife
So I always buy boots three sizes too tight;
The only fun I get is when I take them off at night –
Oh you can't help lookin' on the bright side.

(*I've got piles*, repeat)

> **The Unluckiest Man in the World found that his wife
> had been unfaithful to him twice. Once with the Brig-
> house and Rastrick Brass Band and once with the
> Ninth Gurkha Regiment.**
>
> **The Unluckiest Man in the World collapsed in the
> street and when they took him to hospital and X-rayed
> him, was operated on for a hole-in-the-heart. It was a
> doughnut in his shirt pocket.**

Can't Help Lookin' on the Bright Side

The Unluckiest
Man in the World

'It is the stars, the stars above us govern our condition.'
Shakespeare, *King Lear*

'Shallow men believe in luck.'
Ralph Waldo Emerson

'I make a living.'
Gipsy Rose Lee, as she was getting into her
Rolls Royce

Since the dawn of time, man has looked back into his past and out towards his future and attempted to read either pattern or predisposition in his life. But luck and death both come unasked for like thieves in the night. This is pretty unfortunate since it means that you can't plan your life ahead much beyond tea-time. Also, you can't decide how much luck you're going to have when it eventually arrives. It's no good, for example, having a lot of luck if there is nothing you can do with it. It doesn't matter how much luck you get if you are on a desert island on your own with no ships for a thousand miles. What's the use of walking round the palm trees shouting at the sea, 'God, I feel lucky. Oh, I feel so lucky today?' Also it's no use being lucky if you're not going to have time to use it. For example, what's the use of winning the pools on Monday and dying on Tuesday?

137

A lot of people put credence in charms and amulets. My uncle always said that the first prayer book that was given him by his mother had brought him a lot of luck throughout his life. So he took it about with him for years. Wherever he went, the prayer book went with him. He even slept with it sewn inside his vest. Then one morning they found him dead. He'd been savaged by bookworms.

Below is a short alphabetical guide to the world of luck and fortune-telling.

ALLAH: Allah is a Geordie greeting. For example, 'Allah, hinny, howsit gannin?'

BIRDS OF ILL OMEN: any that ruin your best clothes.

CARTOMANCY: reading carts. This is very hard if the carts are going very fast.

CEPHALOMANCY: reading skulls, In the old days before the invention of paper, information was written down on human skulls and passed round from hand to hand. It was because of this such phrases as 'He's got a good head for figures' came about.

CRYSTAL BALLS: anybody with crystal balls should not stand too near an opera singer with a high soprano voice or you may find it catching.

DEUS EX MACHINA: this is Latin for God's car.

ENTRAILS: reading entrails is a messy business and didn't help Caesar much since his pal Brutus had obviously read them as well. Never try reading your own entrails or your future will be short and predictable. Never eat oysters or go out if there's an Ide in the month.

HANDOMANCY (or *palmistry* as it is known as since it tells the history of your palm): reading palms is relatively simple and can be done by anybody. If the palm is a big one round your throat, the subject is probably angry. If the palm is in your pocket, he or she is probably dishonest. If the palm is in your trouser pocket, and does not belong to you, it's your lucky day. If the palm is in your trouser pocket and it's your own, you'll need glasses eventually.

I CHING: this is a phrase invented by Descartes, the French philosopher, with a pocketful of change, when he coined the immortal words 'I ching, therefore I am.'

THE KRAKEN: the kraken is a legendary bird that lives on the bottom of the sea and is only seen by dead sailors. It is unlucky to see the bird for in order to do so you'd have to be drowned.

MASCOT: mother's bed.

NECROMANCY: conversing with the dead. For example, Tory Party Conferences.

OLD MOORE'S ALMANAC: this is a book that tells you where you can get the best Old Moore's.

PARAPSYCHOLOGY: knowing how to jump out of an aircraft.

PLANTOMANCY: talking to plants. The most dangerous plant to talk to is the deadly nightshirt. This is a poisonous plant, one bite from which results in the instant death of anybody with a Guatamalan Lottery Ticket.

PHRENOLOGY (or *skullomancy*): the art of reading bumps on the head. If the bumps are very big, the person concerned has just had an accident. If they are on the front, he or she has bumped into something. If they are on the back, something has bumped into them. Reading bumps on the chest (or *chestomancy*) is much more interesting.

PORTENT: this is Gaelic for a pauper's dwelling.

PSYCHOKINESIS: is the art of opening sardine tins without a proper opener.

RUNES: casting the runes was a means of fortune-telling typical of the Norsemen, or as they were known, The Yggdrasil. If you could pronounce the name of the tribe Yggdrasil, it was very lucky for you because they then made you chief of the Norsemen, since for 600 years nobody had been able to pronounce it.

SPHINX: Sphinx is the plural of sphincter. These are muscles without which not only would you be unlucky but you would also be very unpopular.

TALISMAN: anybody over 5' 11½''.

TANNINOMANCY: this is the art of reading teacups. If you read Josiah Wedgewood, Etroria Potteries, Stoke-on-Trent on one of your teacups, you're probably quite rich. If you read 'Reject, 10p' you're probably quite poor and will soon meet a tall dark stranger – the bailiff.

WIDDERSHINS: this is an Anglo-Saxon term meaning to bewitch or turn about, from the Anglo-Saxon Widder hinner – to turn. This used to be found as an instruction on Anglo-Saxon road signs.
For example, No Left WIDDERSHINNER.

A LITTLE ZIT ON THE SIDE

Jasper Carrott

He's been a delivery boy (the terror of Solihull), a toothpaste salesman (for four hours), a folkie (repertoire – two songs) – and the most unlikely and original comic superstar for years.

Now Jasper Carrott reveals more of the outrageous talent that has taken him from the Boggery to a series of one-man shows that won him I T V's Personality of the Year Award.

Discover the do-it-yourself man, how to become star of Top of the Pops and the Carrott guide to dog-training. Relive the simple pleasures of The Magic Roundabout, Funky Moped and the Mole.

GULLIBLE'S TRAVELS

Billy Connolly

He has travelled from the majestic deserts of Doha (twin town of Drumchapel in Scotland) and the teeming markets of Bletchley to the splendour of the Sydney surf and the exotic decadence of the Crawley Leisure Centre.

And here it is — a unique guide to the world, travel, life, death and camel-smells, as seen through the eyes of

'the gangling Glaswegian doyen of bad taste' *Daily Telegraph*

'the man who makes Bette Midler look like Jess Conrad' *The Stage*

'one of the most outrageous Scotsmen ever to have vaulted Hadrian's Wall' *Daily Express*

'the laughing laureate of the loo' *The Times*

the inimitable (thank God) BILLY CONNOLLY

Compiled by Duncan Campbell

Illustrated by Steve Bell

Bestselling Humour

ARROW BOOKS, BOOKSERVICE BY POST, PO BOX 29, DOUGLAS, ISLE OF MAN, BRITISH ISLES

NAME ....

ADDRESS ....

....

....

Please enclose a cheque or postal order made out to Arrow Books Ltd. for the amount due and allow the following for postage and packing.

U.K. CUSTOMERS: Please allow 22p per book to a maximum of £3.00.

B.F.P.O. & EIRE: Please allow 22p per book to a maximum of £3.00.

OVERSEAS CUSTOMERS: Please allow 22p per book.

Whilst every effort is made to keep prices low it is sometimes necessary to increase cover prices at short notice. Arrow Books reserve the right to show new retail prices on covers which may differ from those previously advertised in the text or elsewhere.